"A helpful, practical approach n working with youth. I highly rec this handbook as an ongoing resource."

-P.Sanchez Mills, Past Executive Director
of National YWCA, Washington, DC

"I am a social worker and yet, despite all my knowledge...I learned so much from them and felt so supported in what ended up being a far more emotional time for me than I had anticipated."

-C.M. Mental Health Professional and Parent

"They were spot on, especially with mid-brain reactions and really have been helpful filtering our son's reactions. Thank you for your invaluable help."

-L&C, Parents, Germany

"This wonderful guidebook has provided enlightenment and relief for parents that I work with."

-M.Conners, Psychologist

"A practical and mindful approach to raising a teen, and a great guide to keeping the peace while helping them find their way. A must read for parents!"

-M. Higgs, Psychiatrist

"This is a book I have read and reread. The information and examples resonate with both my husband and me. I recommend this book to parents of pre teens, teens and young adults."

-C.Jones, RN, MA Director You and Me.We

"Barbara and Annette presented a topnotch presentation to the parents of Eckerd College first year students. Becoming the parent of a college student is never easy but they offered real tools parents can use throughout a child's entire college career."

-Anne Wetmore, Director of Family &
Student Services, Eckerd College

LAUNCHING

PARENTING TO
COLLEGE & BEYOND

LAUNCHING

Parenting to
College & Beyond

Annette Reiter &
Barbara Rhode

Wasteland Press
Shelbyville, KY USA
www.wastelandpress.net

Launching: Parenting Your Child to College and Beyond
by Annette Reiter and Barbara Rhode

ISBN: 978-1-60047-411-8
First Printing – February 2010

Printed in the U.S.A.

This book is dedicated to our children, Melissa, Ragon, Dylan and Emily, with love and gratitude for all that they teach us.

"Your children are not your children.
They are the sons and daughters of Life's longing for itself.
They come through you but not from you,
And though they are with you yet they belong not to you.
You may give them your love but not your thoughts.
You may house their bodies but not their souls,
For their souls dwell in the house of tomorrow, which you cannot
visit, even in your dreams.
You may strive to be like them,
but seek not to make them like you.
For life goes not backward nor tarries with yesterday.

–"The Prophet," Kahlil Gibran

ACKNOWLEGEMENTS

We are grateful for this opportunity to share our thoughts and ideas with you. Special, heartfelt thanks go to our husbands, who not only encouraged us, but also acted as editors and even publishers as needed. This has been a growth experience for us, and would not have happened without the hard work and patience of our editor, Mary Ellen Collins. Special thanks to the staff and faculty of Eckerd College for their continued support in our endeavors. Most of the wisdom in this handbook comes from the courageous clients who have walked through our doors and shared their stories.

TABLE OF CONTENTS

INTRODUCTION

"You bring up your child to be self-reliant and independent and they double cross you and become self-reliant and independent."
                                        –R.Cormier, *A Bad Time for Fathers*

Let's face it. Parenting even the healthiest adolescent can feel like an endless roller coaster ride. Adolescence is a huge transition for every family member.

After eighteen years of enormous sacrifice and devotion, you find yourself on the cusp of a major letting go process with little or no preparation. Sit back, take a deep breath, and think about what this really means to you, the parent. Remember all those times when you said "no" to invitations, opportunities and adventures because of the money, time or energy they would have taken away from your children. Think hard about all of those some days you must have whispered to yourself. "Someday I will…" "Someday I'll get…" "Someday I'll do…."

Well, don't look now, but someday is finally here! As far as raising your child is concerned, most of the job is done. It's time to let go and "launch" your son or daughter from childhood into young adulthood.* It's time to focus on yourself, your mate, or maybe that new relationship you've been contemplating. It could be the perfect time to recommit to your career or follow a dream you've postponed for years.

As the flight attendants say, "Ladies and gentlemen, the captain has just shut off the seatbelt sign and you are now free to roam around the cabin." Only this time, it is the cabin of your life. But be warned - embracing this new chapter may take some getting used to. It also takes practice in the art of letting go.

To begin this process, step back and ask yourself, "What am I really letting go of?" We're always letting go of something – that's the nature of life. In this case, you might be struggling to let go of hopes and dreams you have held tightly since your son or daughter was very small. You may be attempting to let go of an existing relationship at a time when you're not so sure about what lies ahead. Your child may have struggled and made choices that disappointed you. Now is a good time to work on letting go of that pain, to open up, and practice the art of forgiveness.

Letting go, yours and your child's, is an essential part of the maturation process. It can be painful, but it's definitely necessary for the long-term health of the relationship. We are not very different from the mother bird that pushes the young bird out of the nest, only to swoop down and guard it, keeping all threat away until the young bird proves itself. Eventually, the mother bird allows the young bird to have its independence, letting nature run its course.

Here is your opportunity to let go of the relationship you had with your child, and embrace the new relationship you'll have with your young adult. This process takes time and patience. There will be stops and starts along the way, but hang in there. It's well worth it!

–Barbara and Annette

SECTION ONE

Successful Transition
into Adulthood

CHAPTER ONE

Understanding Young Adult Goals

by Annette Reiter, M.A, L.M.F.T.

"Modeling is not one of the ways we teach others, it's the only way."
—Unknown

C hildren are like sponges that soak up every one of our moves, feelings and actions. Remembering this has helped me focus on the big picture of parenting, which is modeling how to cope with life. I call my daughter a little mirror. When she reflects positive or cute mannerisms, my partner and I give each other that knowing look. When she reflects more annoying traits, we can blame each other as the source of that behavior. Either way, her actions come from us or someone else in her life.

This reflective process may be most clear when children become young adults and the mirror works both ways. Consider these four memory activities that happen when your son drops and breaks a glass, and you yell, "I can't believe you did that!"

- Your son creates a memory of that act, and your reaction.
- Your son stores that memory, and will recall it years later when he's a parent and his child breaks a glass.
- You create a memory of your son's act, and your reaction.
- You remember what happened when you broke a glass, and how your parent reacted.

You're creating these memories subconsciously, but as you launch your child, it will help you to consciously review your own launching history. You may recall some behaviors and pitfalls that you want to avoid. And if you don't identify what you want to avoid, you tend to recreate it.

The preadolescent and adolescent age group tends to either identify with or against their parents. Either way, parents are their defining point and are equally valued regardless of their assigned definition. Adults also do this. When you review your own leaving home experience, you can choose to repeat your parents' actions, or choose to do things differently. This is why it's helpful to do a purposeful review of your own launching history – not to blame, but to understand.

While writing this book, I was reminded of my father, who in his mid- fifties, wrote a book. My teenage, sarcastic reaction at the time was, "I guess you can do just about anything at any age," because he seemed so old to me. I stored that memory and laid down that script. Now, in writing this book, sarcasm has changed to pride as I say, "I can do anything at any age."

You are now in the middle of creating the script of your child's launching. Your actions and your child's actions make up the script he will review twenty-five years from now when he's launching his child.

During this developmental stage, the young adult strives to gain independence from the family. We have all experienced the high wire act of trying to balance this newfound freedom with the innate human need to be connected to a family unit. We leave our family to create a new life, but we don't sever that original family connection. All young adults do this differently, depending on factors including personality type, coping skills, family dynamics, brain development, cultural issues, and health concerns.

I compare the process to climbing stairs. One person may know how to do laundry when she leaves home, so she's standing on the third step. Someone else has no idea how to do it, so he's still on the first step. Either way, all young adults have to go up the staircase.

As parents, our job is to observe and notice, "Are they moving up the staircase?" If they're taking two steps up and one step back, this is still upward momentum. Maybe, they get stuck on a certain stair, i.e., they can't handle their money, they experiment with substances, they struggle with grades or work. All of these can happen during these developmental stages, so you need to be ready to offer encouragement and support as your son or daughter tackles the challenges of balancing new freedoms with family ties.

EXERCISE

Gaining independence from the family eventually involves finding a place to live and learning general life skills, including self-care and fiscal management. Helping your children with this before they leave can be comforting to all of you.

Living within a budget can be overwhelming if you've never created one. Work with your young person on a pretend budget. Pull out your own bills for a month, prorate the number for a single person, and add on the costs of food, entertainment and transportation. Add them up and compare expenses to monthly income.

The more you work on helping your children develop their adult skill sets before they launch, the more confidence you'll have in them. Model patience and remind yourself the goal is independence from the family.

CHAPTER TWO

How Do Their Brains Work?

by Annette Reiter, M.A, L.M.F.T.

"By the time your kids are fit to live with, they live with somebody else."

–Humorist K. Prieskorn

I f you're the caregiver of a child age 15 – 22, you may have asked yourself recently, "Does that kid have a brain?" [11] The answer is, no…well yes, of course he has one, it just isn't fully developed yet. With the advent of new technology and the resulting brain development research, we now know that changes in the frontal and prefrontal cortex occur well into the early 20's.

This is particularly significant for parents of adolescents because this is the part of the brain that controls abstract thinking, impulsivity and emotion. Lack of development in this area decreases a young adult's ability to think strategically, plan behavior, demonstrate cognitive flexibility and regulate emotion.

The seat of emotions lies in the middle brain, which acts as the CEO of the brain until the frontal cortex is fully formed. This means that emotions are ruling behavior in your teens and young adults. Because they do not have a fully wired frontal cortex to kick in, they stay in

---

[1] Norvell, Walter – Quote and subsequent topic are adapted from article Inside the Adolescent Brain

their emotional middle brain and as a result, can be terribly reactive. They're likely to have emotional outbursts, and they're perfectly hard wired for power struggles.

Coercive or threatening behavior actually appeals to and stimulates the middle brain, so you'll find that non-threatening consequences are more effective when dealing with this age group. Don't be accusatory or condescending, or says things like, "What's wrong with you?!" Instead, use statements like, "Let's think this through," or "What steps have you taken to deal with this?"

The crazy outbursts and quick emotional changes stress out the teens as much as they do their parents. I had one young client who described a happy, fun, loving relationship with her mother. The next week, she described the relationship as one that disgusted her. Her mother now revolted her and she proclaimed herself as "dis-attracted" to her mother. After reminding her of how she had felt the previous week, she said she was aware of the extreme difference and couldn't make sense of it herself. She hated herself for feeling this way. This roller coaster of emotions is not gender specific – I've heard the same tale from many young boys as well.

This is what leads teenagers and young adults to feeling misunderstood.[2] They don't even understand themselves. What we used to attribute to puberty, we now view as normal brain development.

Additionally, teens process information differently than adults. Research shows that teens read faces incorrectly, regularly mistaking "fear or surprise" for "anger".[3] Think about a time when your son said something that made you react fearfully or with surprise.

He would read your reaction as being angry. Since most parents of teenagers are in a constant state of fear or surprise during this roller coaster period, it's no wonder teenagers regularly proclaim, "You hate me," to their parents.

---

[2] Nelson, Charles – PBS Frontline Interview
[3] Megan, K. – Article Touching Off Teen Tantrum

If you've ever caught yourself thinking, "She'd forget her head if it wasn't attached," know that you're dealing with a lack of frontal cortex development. In general, the regulating parts of the brain, frontal/prefrontal cortex and the corpus collosum, do not appear to be totally formed until 20 years of age or older. The corpus collosum is the nerve bundle that connects the two sides of the brain. Without this connection parents can anticipate experiencing a decreased development of intelligence, consciousness, and self-awareness. Give it time, they are building an adult brain.

So how is it that they remember their dates or to call their girl/boyfriends yet they can't call home when they're late for curfew and they forget their homework regularly? Without the pre-frontal cortex to offer up any reasoning or regulate emotions, the hypothalamus takes over and remembers all details related to their special love relationship. The pre-frontal cortex tends to settle the hypothalamus down, as the hypothalamus is "in love with being in love".[4]

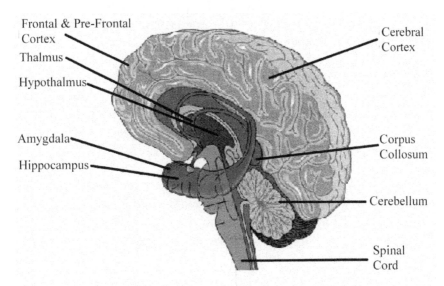

Website – image adapted from the site: http://www.math.tudresden.de/~belov/brain/humbrain2.gif

---

[4] Norvell, Walter –From the article Inside the Adolescent Brain

Many young adults think their parents don't understand this kind of feeling. From their perspective, adults take all the passion out of relationships. But as silly as they look to you, with their constant IM's and 200 text messages a day, you look just as silly to them without all that technology.

The hypothalamus also controls survival functions, including the fight or flight response, which is why parents of young adults frequently report that all their kid seems to do is pick a fight or sulk away.[5] They talk back, hang up on you, and slam doors. Although this can be an extremely rocky time, remember that behavior that looks crazy on the surface is actually a sign of normal brain development.

Additionally, in the process of the frontal and prefrontal cortex formation, the brain goes in and wipes out some of the weaker connections. This wipe out can take place up to 3 times in the normal teen and young adult years, causing distress in both parents and kids.

Your teen may be remembering things, acting responsible, and even making good choices ... when out of the blue, he starts acting several years younger. It's like a switch got turned off. This may be caused by one of these brain wipes.

I've had young adults in tears in my office over forgetting something that was very important to them. I remind myself, them and their parents that setbacks are to be expected; and people tend to come back stronger after a setback. Remember, we're creating people here – complex people – it really shouldn't be easy.

I often tell my teenage clients about how I looked forward to turning sixteen. I was going to drive a car everywhere and have a more grown up body, but I never dreamed of the responsibilities that came with being sixteen – making dating decisions, getting a job, getting good grades, and planning for college.

Every additional year brings more independence, and the great equalizer, more responsibilities. A parent's job is to balance responsibility and independence. Giving a young adult too much

[5] Norvell, Walter – Topic is adapted from the article Inside the Adolescent Brain

independence without responsibility may lead to a spoiled adult who struggles with working hard and having drive. Giving too much responsibility with little independence can lead to a resentful adult who is always overburdened and has little joy in life.

Parents regulate a child's independence by the amount of responsibility they give him. And now you understand that a young person can't demonstrate responsibility beyond their level of brain development. So take this blueprint to help you figure out where you need to focus your efforts by coaching, encouraging, and supporting your son or daughter.

EXERCISE

Ask your child to imagine that he could go back in time and meet himself at a younger age. Ask him to explain to the younger self how things are going to change in five years. He will quickly discover that some things are unexplainable to his younger self.

Then ask him to imagine going into the future and meeting his 23-year-old self. What does he imagine that the older self will tell him? Eventually, some of the same difficulties in explanation will develop, and he'll discover that you're simply not ready for some things until you get there.

Remind him that parents have some idea of what might be in store for him, and they are trying to prepare him for the future without giving him more information than he needs at the time.

CHAPTER THREE

Seeing Things Differently

by Annette Reiter, M.A, L.M.F.T.

"A child's job is to test her boundaries; a parent's is to see that she survives the test."

–Dr. Roger MacDonald

Now that you have some insight into how your young person's brain is developing, it may help you to view their behavior through a different lens. This isn't an easy time for them, and although their actions may alarm or upset you, the reality may be that they're doing exactly what they're supposed to be doing at this stage.

For example, your son refuses to clean his room, and you label this refusal as "laziness." But, his behavior may actually be a reflection of his struggle for independence, which is perfectly normal. He may not feel ready to take on some older responsibilities, so he's trying to get you to step in and take over things that he should be responsible for.

Looking at something from a new angle can give you some relief while offering insight into your child's behavior.

Talking back and not showing respect are signs that your young adult is trying on the "power role," which can cause friction between you. He's trying to gain power in relationships, because you have had most of the power up to this point. We've already talked about the brain chemistry that makes him act the way he does, so it may also help you to deal with the friction better when you realize that his behavior stems from confusion about power and adulthood.

Children experience their caregivers as powerful, so naturally they see power as a part of adult life. As they try to gain power by using a less-than-respectful tone of voice, they're practicing on the person who will never leave them, i.e., you. OUCH! Seeing this for what it is may not help with the sting, but it may change your emotional reaction to this behavior.

Lying is another common behavior that may send you right off the deep end. Your daughter tells you she went to school, and a neighbor says she saw her hanging out at the mall when she should've been in class. You react emotionally and jump to worst case scenarios: How could I have raised a child who would lie? If she's lying about this, what else is she lying about?

Instead of leaping to negative conclusions, ask, "Could there be a constructive purpose for her lying?" Remind yourself that at one time or another, everybody lies. Some people have to learn by doing – your daughter might be lying in order to figure out the dynamics of lying. If she has always figured things out by jumping into them, the consequences of her actions will teach her what's right and what's wrong.

Think about why you don't lie anymore. It's because something inside you says that lying isn't acceptable, and it won't make you feel good about yourself. Where did you get this internal moral compass? Even if lying in some cases might be easier – your internal gauge stops you.

Your teen is in the process of developing her own internal gauge. If you confront her with her lie, express your viewpoint, but don't take on her emotional shame. Young adults need to learn to carry and internalize their own disappointment. Put the burden back on her without having an accusatory reaction. If she says, "Aren't you going to get mad at me?" respond with, "It's your life. You get to screw it up and you get to pay the price."

Even if you can't avoid that initial explosive reaction, you can always revisit the subject. Feel free to go back, hours... days... even weeks later, and explain that your reaction was wrong; you're not really mad at her. You're sad for her and the choice she made. You still talk to her about the problem, but come at it from a different angle and a different energy that she will be more likely to hear.

Sometimes, there may even be a constructive purpose to lying for young adults. A good example of this is when your child promises you that he won't go to parties where alcohol is served to minors. I've had numerous teen clients who make that promise, and then go to the party, but they don't drink.

If you ask, "Why don't you just tell your parents that you go, but you don't drink, they quickly respond, 'Because then I would have to drink.'"

This makes no logical sense to most adults because we don't look at it from a self-test perspective. The young adult who does this is testing himself to find out if he can keep a limit without it being set by his parents. If he can't, he can always return to the safer boundary set by mom and dad. This is a form of trying on adult behaviors and skills with the safety net that, my parents boundary is just one step back.

Young adults also do this when they say, "No, my parents won't let me go to a midnight rap concert" without ever having asked their parent for permission! They don't know how to set limits on their own, so they use their parents as a shield. Part of this developmental stage is learning how to say "no" alone. It's just another way that they're practicing the use of adult behaviors and skills.

Anticipate friction, lies, stress and frustration ... but try to step outside your own emotional box. Adjust your perspective, look for the developmental changes behind the behavior, and remember that they're learning how to be grown-ups.

EXERCISE

Imagine that your child is in a dress rehearsal for a great Broadway premier of "My Life," and you are her director. Assume that she's an inexperienced actress, and her screw-ups try your patience. You can't fire her because she fits the role perfectly, so you have to redirect her, give her better lines, and create ways for her to be successful in a quality production.

Different parents have come up with the most interesting ways of implementing this idea. One of my favorites is the mother who made a loud, obnoxious buzzer sound every time her teenage daughter was rude or disrespectful. Then she calmly said, "Stop, think, rewrite," and instructed her daughter to go think about what she had just said, and to come back later to do it differently. Eventually, they both started to laugh when they heard the buzzer. The mother experienced a decrease in stress by not accepting everything out of her daughter's mouth as the final cut; and her daughter seemed relieved to be able to edit her remarks and try again.

Get creative about what technique would work in your family. One father of a college student decided to say, "You may want to think about that, you could see it differently later. Let's talk then." Eventually, this turned into, "Let's talk later." This father reported that his son would sometimes even apologize!

CHAPTER FOUR

Teens, Technology & Parenting Trends

by Annette Reiter, M.A, L.M.F.T.

"The most important question is not what the Internet will do to us but what we will do with it"

–Robert Putnam, "Bowling Alone"

Breathe. Seriously, take a deep breath. If you are parenting a child between the ages of 15 and 25 today, you may need to take a deep breath every two to three minutes while they're around. If you're like many overstressed, overcommitted parents today, you may be tempted to take the easy way out when dealing with your children, and opt for "buying peace at any price." Unfortunately, that's just what you get - peace at any price. And too often, that price is that our children don't learn about boundaries, limits, and skill sets they'll need as adults.

Over the last two decades, many parents adopted a parenting style fueled by experts who were very concerned about children's self esteem. They encouraged us to support and encourage our children, and to go as far as making them feel like "winners" even when they didn't put forth any effort at all. To be clear, this is not just spoiling them with stuff, but with a failure to set limits, (thereby making them ill prepared to handle the real limits of adult life.) Fast forward 10-20 years and we now have a generation called the Millenials, who think pretty highly of themselves but lack the emotional calluses to see them through the inevitable tough times. A few years ago, a tearful

25-year-old came to my office, sure that something was wrong with him. He had been "crying off and on for a week, and was wondering if he was depressed." The cause of the emotional meltdown was the fact that his first boss, in his first job, had told him to be on time for meetings and work every day. This, after he missed a meeting "because he just didn't think it was that important." I wish I could tell you this was an unusual case, but unfortunately, it has become the norm.

Many experts are calling these millenials and their parents, "generation stressed". Fear and stress levels have drastically increased for everyone since 9/11. One third of American children suffer from stress related symptoms, one half of adolescents have trouble sleeping and one in two college students are so overwhelmed they have trouble sleeping. Our instant gratification culture helps to fuel rising stress levels in kids who, according to 80% of Americans are more spoiled today than ever. These Companies have been marketing to millenials since they were toddlers, and this generation now views more than 40,000 commercials a year. Parents not only spoil them by giving them stuff, but also by not helping them to develop the skills and sense of responsibility they'll need as independent adults. According to Gail Ryser, a PhD at the University of Texas "Our children are missing out on learning how to want for things, earn things and overcome obstacles to get what they want."

Whenever a skill set is incongruent with age, stress is likely to increase, either in the form of depression or anxiety. Jean Twenge, in "Generation Me" calls the millenial experience "a time of soaring expectations and crushing realities." Many experts agree, predicting this may be the first generation in this country's history to graduate and earn less than their parents, and also to have a shorter lifespan. It isn't hard to understand why even millenials, with their inflated ego, may become more depressed and anxious than any other coming of age generation.

This pattern is part of a larger social issue of declining connectedness. Robert Putnam discusses this in his book "Bowling Alone", observing that although more Americans are bowling than ever before, participation in league bowling has plummeted in the last 10 to 15 years. He concludes that Americans are suffering from declining social capital unlike any generation before. This social crisis has transgressed into our homes, with Technology being partly to blame. Research from the University of Minnesota clearly states that in families that have TV's in the bedroom, children were less physically active, had poor dietary habits, ate fewer family meals together and had poor school performance.

In a recent UCLA study from the Center on Everyday Lives of Family, researchers mapped the locations of family members every 10 min on GPS and found that family members were only in the same room as another family member 16% of the time. "While we have been miraculously connecting electronically over the past fifteen years, we have also quietly and unintentionally been disconnecting interpersonally," says Dr. Edward Hallowell. With access to so many fast paced technologies, it's not hard to see how we've become a generation of instant gratification. Hallowell details the agony of waiting for a rotary dial phone to connect while on vacation with his family, in his book "Crazy Busy". He defines "suffering from modern life" as having symptoms of being "overbooked and about to snap" or in the "F-state...frantic, frenzied, forgetful, flummoxed, frustrated and fragmented." I know firsthand that after carpooling to school, various lessons, exercise class for myself, working one night a week for both my husband and myself, co-op sorting, shopping, doing laundry, caring for my geriatric dog, phone calls covering concerns for my aging out-of-town parents and more and more and more...by Wednesday of any given week, I fit all and sometimes another one of the "F-state" words.

But what should we do and how can we make life better for our children? Getting rid of TV, cell phones, and computers seems rather extreme, and isn't likely to help. I don't want to be rid of these tools. I think progressive technologies are here to stay and more are to come. Like it or not, we have become a nation of quick fixes and it's from this platform that we must learn, teach and model balance. This is the new form of citizenship we must model, "Digital Citizenship". Adults must join the world that children operate in or else they are left to their own devices to figure things out. What used to happen in an ice cream parlor or downtown strip on Friday or Saturday night, now takes place in a virtual world with limited adult supervision to teach and model manners, values and good behavior.

But what are we up against? Facebook, MySpace, Flickr, YouTube, Wikipedia, TV, IPODS, Cell phones and more. It's enough to make you want to text OMG TMA. (Oh, my gosh, too many acronyms!). The advancements in technology, combined with certain cultural changes may have created the perfect storm in which adults may be more important to this next generation than ever. And it may be time to take a gentle approach and model balance by being open to change ourselves. For example many parents may be in awe of our children's skill and comfort with technological advances. My 8 year old understands and works our new digital camera, navigates my cell phone and loads new programs onto our family computer better than I do. Yikes! (Insert deep breaths here). So why not invite your child to teach you to text or get on Facebook or write a blog? Then you teach them to discuss literature, explore wildlife or make dinner. Ok, I know some of you are cringing at the "discuss literature idea" but there are some really great novels, movies and plays about coming of age. Maybe you could form a group with other like minded parents, and get together with your kids to talk about what you've read or seen together. It may inspire them to see adulthood as somewhat fun and exciting. It could happen!

Accept the reality that stress is a part of life in the 21st century and make a conscious effort to arm your children with the skills necessary to navigate the stressful world. Model a balanced diet of technology in your own life and teach them manners that apply in both virtual and real worlds. Giving them everything they want, or allowing them to believe they're entitled to everything they want, is not what they need. Allowing them to live life glued to technological device isn't the answer either. Set limits and boundaries, teach them how to cope with disappointment, and show through your own example the importance of balancing the joys of technology with the joys of interpersonal connection. Creating a new model may take risk on your part, but think of the risks they're facing as they make the sometimes rocky transition to adulthood. Then jump right in and get started!

EXERCISE

Make a list of current technologies you and your children currently use and the amount of time spent on each. Also make a list of ways you do (or could) practice real connection with others in your community. Then go to work on both.

Here are some ideas:

Technology
Cell Phone (calling, texting)
Computer (email, instant messaging, blogging)
iPod or mp3 player
Wii, Xbox or other system

Community Connections
Garden or Book Club
Cooking Classes
Theatre, Music, Movies
Discussion Groups
Family Game Night
Volunteer Time
Progressive Dinners
Picnics with Others

Cyberbullying

Many parents have concerns about cyberbullying. I also encourage them to be proactive and get involved in technology with their child. Additionally, please read and enact the "Top Ten Tips" for preventing and responding to Cyberbullying at *www.cyberbullying.us* Other great information can be found at *www.stopcyberbullying.org*

CHAPTER FIVE

Supporting the Journey

by Annette Reiter, M.A, L.M.F.T.

"When you give your children knowledge...you are telling them what to think. When you give your children wisdom, rather than telling them what to think, you are telling them how to find their own truth."

–Unknown

Wisdom-building can be challenging for parents and children. This phase of life requires courage, energy, a tolerance for ambiguity, and a strong willingness to take risks.

On Donald Trump's "The Apprentice" TV show several years ago, the winning team got to spend an evening at a piano bar with Billy Joel. Some of these 21-23 year-olds didn't even know who Billy Joel was, but eventually one of them asked what advice he had for someone young, who was just starting out.

Billy took a long pause and finally said, "Go into the world brave." He explained that the world might not always be kind to you, or like you, and that it takes a lot of strength to realize your dreams.

I tell this story because I think it's very good advice for young adults, and an excellent reminder to parents about how much strength it takes to grow up.

Growing up involves an ability to face fear with courage, and courage rarely feels courageous while you're experiencing it. Most people in the middle of being courageous report feeling like they've made the biggest mistake of their lives. This is natural. Think back to times of courage in your life and ask yourself what you were feeling. You were probably riddled with self-doubt, second-guessing every move, exhausted, and an emotional wreck. This sounds like most young adults I meet.

Remember this when dealing with your own young person. Tame your critical voice, since he's probably already pretty down about himself.

Use yourself and your problems to model accountability, responsibility and insight to your child. You probably figure out solutions to hundreds of problems a day, but you do it so automatically now you have forgotten the steps. Remember when you were parenting a baby? You walked around talking out loud about everything because this is how babies learn language.

Sit down with your young adult and discuss a situation that's causing you trouble today. Highlight the steps you're going through. It may not be a big deal to you, but remember that she isn't as experienced in step-by-step problem solving. It may seem like she isn't listening or doesn't care, but that is not your concern. Your job is to plant seeds; her job is to grow them.

When your daughter is trying to make a decision or figure something out, offer encouragement and support, but not answers. Say things like: "You can do it." "That sounds like a tough problem – I know you can figure that out." "Let me know how it works out." "How did you do that?" Ask the questions even when you know the answers.

Helping your child to build wisdom is letting her chart her own course; supporting her journey without leading her every step of the way.

EXERCISE

Read "Please Understand Me" by David Keirsay. It includes a shortened version of the Myers/Briggs personality test, which all members of the family can take. The test is made up of easy questions, and your answers reveal how you:

- gather energy to refuel yourself
- gather information and choose what to focus on
- make decisions
- relate to the world around you

Families enjoy finding out what everyone's "type" is. No one type is better than another, and each has advantages and disadvantages. All personality types can accomplish goals, make good decisions and find peacefulness.

Gaining insight into your similarities and differences can help you determine the most effective way to support your child and help him build wisdom.

SECTION TWO

Successful Transition
From Parent to Coach

CHAPTER SIX

Navigating the 'Letting Go' Path

by Barbara Rhode, M.S., L.M.F.T.

"What the caterpillar thinks is the end of the world, the butterfly knows is only the beginning."

—Anonymous

Launching your child won't be the easiest journey you ever take, but we can offer a few tips to smooth the way.

Resist the urge to control

The nature of the parenting process turns most adults into authority figures. Raising young children puts you in the driver's seat, a necessary position for their survival and well-being. But refusing to relinquish control as your child matures can cause problems. As children grow up, they want and deserve incremental amounts of autonomy. But some parents, out of fear, refuse to make the shift, creating problems for everyone.

When acting as authority figures, we tell our children what to do and we expect their compliance. We're expected to have the answers, and in the event that we don't, we seek out an expert to advise us. This parenting style includes giving orders and is built on the dynamics of control and power. We act as our children's "boss," and they listen to us because we know better.

If you've used this style for most of your child's life, take some time to evaluate how well this has worked. Systematic Training for Effective Parenting by Don Dinkmeyer and Gary McKay is a valuable resource if you need some assistance in this area.

A parental coaching style evolves from the belief that the power in the relationship should be shared. This doesn't mean that the parent loses all authority. You can still set limits and boundaries, but you treat your child as a young adult in the making, with all the respect and autonomy she deserves.

The parent as coach is an empathetic mentor, making suggestions, sharing information and listening to your young person's concerns and issues. You can admit to him that the two of you do not agree on a particular issue. You can point out the pros and cons and then step back while he tries to sort through this. You are there to give advice, not to be the one with all the answers!

This style of parenting teaches the young person to think on his own and take responsibility for his actions. The parent is there, like the mother bird, to perform damage control and maximize the young one's ability to survive and thrive. The young person, not the parent, is responsible for the outcome.

For example, shortly after one of our workshops, a mom called to tell us that as she was driving back home after leaving her son at his dorm, her cell phone rang. It was her newly launched son, highly agitated because he had already lost his cell phone. She took a breath, and asked herself, "Whose problem is this?" Practicing her newly heightened sense of detachment, she handed the problem back to her son, saying, "Oh, that's terrible. What are you going to do?" He was a little shocked at her response, but managed to say, "I guess I'm gonna call the cell phone company." He did have to ask for the number, but she was very proud of herself for moving from the role of "rescuer" to that of "coach."

Even if you've already handed over power to your young person, this is a good time to relinquish even more. When issues come up, ask yourself, 'Whose problem is this, anyway?' If it's your child's and nine times out of ten it will be, step away and let her handle it. However, beware of subtle manipulations. Some young people may try to get you to take the steering wheel again, actually prefer to leave you in the driver's seat, or at least try to let you believe that you are still in control.

But if you choose to stay there, what will your young person learn? She'll learn that you don't believe she's capable of handling her own problems or that you will always be there to rescue her when she falls down. Are those the lessons you want to teach her?

Confront your fears

Many of our decisions as parents have been fear-based. That's easy to understand when you step back and look at the messages we're being flooded with in the news.

There are a lot of frightening things out there, but ask yourself if fear-based decisions are sound decisions. Do they direct your young person to where he needs to be?

As a nation, we are immobilized by the possibility of child abduction, which actually only happens to one out of 1,300,000 children, annually.[67] And yet, we routinely ignore the risk of heart disease, which regularly happens to 1 out of every 300 adults. Refuse right now to make any more decisions based on fear.

Remind yourself that the ultimate goal is to assist your young person in this important separation and individuation process. It may seem like he just keeps falling in the mud again and again, but don't our most profound life lessons come with a little dirt on them?

I bruised myself a few times as a young adult, and that bruising taught me some essential life lessons that I still use today. Why would we want to cheat our children out of any of these valuable

---

6 Parade Magazine, March 30, 2003

experiences? Who will they become as adults if they don't learn from their own mistakes?[78]

As parents, we have to face our own fears and ask ourselves, "Who am I really trying to protect?" The only way for us to handle fear is to face it squarely as an impartial observer, not as an engaged co-conspirator. Practice observing your fears. Look deep inside yourself and watch as fear rears up over some issue your young person presents. Purposely, without letting it pull you in and create a reaction, let the fear dissipate. Your children will benefit more from watching you model effectively handling your own fears than from countless lectures or rescue attempts. Other than your unconditional love, there is probably no greater gift you can give them.

Know that stress is normal

Go ahead – accept right up front that this normal, developmental process is stressful. Even positive changes that we choose and eagerly anticipate trigger the body's natural stress hormones. If you have ever taken one of those life event surveys, you've seen that even happy events, such as weddings and births, receive a significant number of stress points.

Understanding up front that stress goes hand-in-hand with launching a young adult will make you feel less confused and guilty. Know that there will be some pain or discomfort in the process, and nurture yourself before the signs and symptoms of 'distress' start to show. By anticipating it, you can reduce the harmful physical and emotional effects the stress can have on each of you.

Launching a child is not a painless process, but has parenthood ever really been painless? You are separating yourself from someone you love deeply, while reprocessing many of the hopes and dreams you secretly (and not so secretly) cultivated for years. You've probably spent the majority of the last 18 years feeding your young person the

---

[7] Information adapted from
http://www.americancatholic.org/messenger/Aug2002/Feature3.asp

best you had, and now you have to tell yourself, "Job well done, prepare to disengage."

Trust that some of what you have said and taught has been heard, and believe that you are still your young person's most significant role model. The research tells us that even with all the additional stimulation and exposure our children receive, parents remain their most important mentors and teachers.

EXERCISE

By learning simple "belly breathing," which is adapted from yoga teachings, you have a valuable tool to use when your muscles start to tense up and the stress feels overwhelming.

Place your hand over your belly button and take a deep breath in through your nose. Try to be aware of the slight swell as you inhale. Hold the breath for the count of three, and then, slowly release through your mouth. Be aware of your hand as it moves back against your abdomen, gently releasing as much air as possible from your lungs. Allow your shoulders to drop a little as you exhale, enhancing the relaxation effects. Repeat the breath until you begin to feel more relaxed. You'll be amazed at the difference ten good breaths can make!

CHAPTER SEVEN

Slippery Slopes

by Barbara Rhode, M.S., L.M.F.T.

"A balanced foundation comes with the desire to grow up, show up, and take your place in life."

—Choquette

B lind spots between our child and ourselves can complicate the launching process, tripping us up just when we think we've perfected our version of the separation dance. If you're aware of these slippery slopes ahead of time, you can recognize the signs and steer around them.

Buying into their thought system

The brain is undergoing intense change and upheaval just when young people most require logical thinking and clarity. Your 17-year-old son, who was always known in the family as the dependable one, suddenly seems to have trouble remembering where his head is and what he should be doing with it. Your 19-year old daughter can recite all of her friends' cell phone numbers but she can't remember to pick up a gallon of milk.

It's a neurological fact that there is a lot of hidden reconstruction and renovation going on in their heads. So why do some of us react so quickly when they call home that first semester screaming hysterically about the latest crisis with their roommates?[8] We don't help matters by adding another emotional reaction into the mix.

Many of the urgent phone calls home that first year will probably include the word, roommate. Living with another person, even someone their own age who might have looked 'perfect' at first glimpse, can present a challenging dynamic.

The good news is that this time – it doesn't include you. For once, all of that angst and drama is not directed at you or another family member.

This is your young adult's biggest and best opportunity to learn the art of compromise, conflict resolution and appropriate boundary setting. Here is your chance to practice being the parental coach, by listening, being empathetic, and saying things like, "I understand." "What are you planning to do about this?" and "I can only imagine how you must have felt but how do you think he or she was feeling at that moment?"

Granted, you will need to step in if the roommate actually poses a threat to your child's safety, but in 99% of roommate crises, this isn't the case. Your new coaching role involves assessing the level of trouble this collegiate stranger poses to your child, and acting accordingly.

Practice the fine art of disengaging, and step back from getting involved in anything other than a real emergency. This is a prime time for your son or daughter to begin to deal with the realities of life outside of your home while in the relative safety of the college dorm.

And while you're at it, be honest with yourself. Don't you feel a small sense of satisfaction that some of those nasty habits your child perfected under your watch are now causing problems for them with their roommates?

Isn't it a challenge to bite your tongue and resist the urge to blurt out, "I told you so?"

---

[8] Fee, Susan - "My Roommate is Driving Me Crazy!"

Staying out of the sandbox

We all have a few favorite "poor me" stories we like to tell anyone who will listen. Hang around me long enough and you will eventually hear about the time my daughter said to my neighbor, Susan, "You're the mother I never had." The problem with these stories is that they are negative and fear-based, and they keep us stuck in patterns of behavior we say we want to change.

So, when your son begins to tell you about a bad grade he received, you might find yourself reacting the same way you always have. Your replay the broken record about what a failure as a parent you are—and you know you won't qualify as a perfect parent unless you jump right into the sandbox with your child, call the professor, and try to resolve grade issue.

This is the perfect time to detach from all that noise in your head, stay out of the sandbox, and listen to your son's explanation about the grade.

A dramatic change in grades can be important if it's a symptom of a larger problem. If your son cannot or will not explain a sudden grade decline, then you might begin to explore what else is going on. A profound drop in grades can be an indication of excessive partying, drug use, or a sign of depression.

Most of the time, however, there's a simple explanation – he was late in turning in a paper that was worth a big chunk of the grade, or he didn't realize the library was closed on the day he was planning to do his research. The next set of grades will reflect the shift or adjustment he made in order to improve grades.

Repeat after me, "Their grades are never, ever my responsibility." They are, however, another important opportunity for your child to grow up and handle a challenge. And, by the way, when did we decide that everyone had to get good grades all the time? We seem to have become a society that is intolerant of poor grades, as if our children deserve only A's and cannot possibly learn a valuable lesson or two from a C, a D, or even an F!

So, when that old fear of failure (yours or theirs) emerges, resist the urge to jump in the sandbox. When you step in to rescue your children, you are inadvertently sending the message that you don't really believe they can handle problems effectively on their own. Instead, coach them in the fine art of effective communication with professors, or help them to improve their study habits. These skills will benefit them far longer than any parentally manipulated grade.

Whose money is it, anyway?

College tuition has gone up significantly in the past few years, and most parents are keenly aware of the sacrifices they had to make in order to send a child to school. This investment can begin to carry some hidden costs, such as the parental feeling that your child "owes" you something in return.

If you're carrying around any hidden agendas like this, try not to dump them on your child. The subtle expectation that your daughter "owes" it to you to become a success can contaminate the new adult relationship you are trying to develop. If you do notice these feelings, be honest with yourself and talk them over with someone you trust. These complicated feelings are more about you than they ever will be about your young adult.

And what about the issue of a monthly allowance? Is it fair to expect your son to work part time during that first year away, or do you underwrite all of his expenses, even dumping money into that virtual vacuum called extracurricular activities?

Money issues can easily lead to conflict. In most relationships, one partner tends to be more of the spender and the other more of a saver, so that leaves plenty of room for disagreements on the parental front. Mom might agree with the daughter who complains that she needs more spending money, and dad might feel that mom is being too lenient.

Newsweek reported in May, 2006 that 17% of college students receive a monthly allowance from their parents averaging $869 and that 14% of the students turn to mom or dad to help them settle credit card debts while in school.[910]

Credit card companies are even opening offices on college campuses, offering cards to students who have no clue about how to manage this new privilege and what level of charges their parents would consider to be reasonable.

Approximately 54% of college freshmen and 90% of sophomores carry at least one credit card with an average balance of about $2,300 a month. Many students are now graduating from college not only with degree, but also with a poor credit rating. The average debt a college student graduates with is $20,000 and that's not all from student loans.

It's not too late to educate your young adult on the pluses and minuses of credit card use. One good website for this is www.creditcardnation.com.

In matters of money as with everything else, the parental coach has to step back and ask, "What is in my young adult's best interest?" There are no one-size-fits-all answers to these questions because every child and every situation is different. You can always adjust your decision once you hear new information or your child demonstrates improved money-handling skills.

Keep your eye on the goal – to enable your young adult to become self sufficient, healthy and independent.

---

[9] Newsweek, "Money Guide: A Cash Course for Kids" September 12, 2005

EXERCISE

Use these questions to create a plan of action that will best suit your young person:

1. What are your expectations concerning his spending, pocket money, and extra cash? What are his expectations?

2. Is it in my son's best interest to focus solely on school or would it actually benefit him more to maintain a part time job while attending school?

3. How has he handled money in the past? Has he been able to save any or does it consistently burn a hole in his pocket?

4. When you warned him this past summer that he needed to save for this upcoming dry spell, how did he react?

The answers to these questions will help you formulate a plan for avoiding that disturbing phone call in which your young adult tells you he's gone through all of his allocated funds in the third week of a very long semester!

Failure is Not a
Four Letter Word

by Barbara Rhode, M.S., L.M.F.T.

"Adversity introduces a man to himself"

–Anonymous

T he process of making a decision, especially a difficult one, is different for everyone. When I look back at my own decision-making process, I realize that it has changed radically from the time I was young. Like you, I have accumulated a variety of life experiences that have given me a broad foundation on which to base my decisions. Most parents have quite a repertoire of diverse situations and events to pull from, but our adolescent and young adult children have a much more limited scope of experience against which they can measure an issue.

How do we help the young people around us learn to make wise and sound decisions? One of the most important ways is to step back and allow them to learn through occasional failures. Last year, Newsweek magazine featured a set of interviews with a group of young people they considered to be very successful. I read the interviews to see if there was a prominent theme. It was the theme of failure. Most of the young men and women said they had been lucky enough to grow up in a home with parents who let them fail, while continuing to support them emotionally and encourage them unconditionally. Some of them said they'd been able to learn a great deal from their mistakes, and that they grew to appreciate and value that parenting style.

As parental coaches, we are engaged in "people building", a long, slow process. A key part of the coach's job description is to watch our young people trip and fall, and then encourage them to stand back up, brush themselves off and give it another try. If we ran to assist our toddlers every time they fell, crawling behind them to ensure their safety, they might have never learned to walk. Instead, most of us stood by wincing when they did fall, and trying to prevent only the really big accidents.

One of my colleagues says that parenting is all about damage control. It's our job to use wisdom and sound judgment in discerning when to step in and when to stay out.

Healthy risk taking is a normal, essential part of adolescent development. Teens and young adults who take risks "...are 20% more likely than teens who do not to avoid alcohol and drugs." (www.acacamps.org). The maturing brain is wired for a certain amount of risk taking. Children have to feel secure in themselves and in the unconditional respect and support of their families in order to take risks and face the chance of failing. Parents who base the building of their children's self-esteem on getting A's, winning trophies, and achieving other successes don't provide enough room and energy for the courage it takes to fail.

Many parents are invested in preventing even a hint of failure from touching children's lives. They will do whatever it takes to quickly wash away failure's inevitable consequences. Research shows us that this approach actually breeds insecurity and a heightened fear of failure in our young people. Taking healthy risks and then learning valuable lessons from the outcomes and their consequences leads to the development of self control and self discipline.

Our children deserve to fail. We failed at times, didn't we? Although my wish as a mother is that my children's failures never become life-altering events, there is no guarantee. Sometimes, the biggest letdowns carry the most growth potential. They can be huge wake-up calls that become effective backdrops against which we look at ourselves and our choices.

My failures ultimately taught me what I did and did not want to do. They also taught me to be more careful during the decision making process by seeking out trusted people who could advise me when I needed it.

We need to equip our children with the tools they will need to "say no, alone" when the time comes. We want them to be able to stand on their own two feet and voice their opinions, even when they are surrounded by peers whose voices sound very different.

Using praise as a reward can be appropriate, but when children earn praise only for winning, it teaches the value of pleasing others and being number one. There is usually an undercurrent of judgment in most forms of praise, even if that judgment is temporarily in the child's favor.

In comparison, think about the benefits of giving encouragement for ongoing effort and hard work, and not for the achievement of a successful outcome. Recent research with Asian families whose children have been valedictorians and scholarship winners noted that encouragement is a key parenting principle in their culture. These parents habitually notice and compliment their children's efforts and the improvements they make, demonstrating their belief in the young person's ability to overcome obstacles.

Allowing our children the freedom to fail, while complimenting them for their efforts rather than their outcomes, leads to a healthy self-image based on reality rather than an inflated ego. And learning from one's mistakes develops the self-confidence that helps to form the perfect foundation for wise decision-making.

EXERCISE

The next time your child is facing an issue and trying to determine what to do about it, use this set of questions to help him or her through the decision making process. For example, say your child is in school, has a part time job on the weekend, and wants to take another job during the week. The process might go like this:

*What are you willing to do? What are you not willing to do?
(By asking these types of questions, you are helping your child begin to evaluate limit setting, exploring boundaries that will keep him/her safe.)

–I am willing to have less free time and a more hectic schedule. I'm not willing to work every single day - I need to be able to get my studying done.

*What do you want to get out of this?
(Now you are assisting them in beginning to define their intention which will guide them consciously and unconsciously.)

–I am trying to figure out a way to make more money without overloading myself.

*What is this for?
(This highlights the purpose behind their action which walks them through a process adults tend to take for granted. It is important to remember that they are still under construction in a neurological sense and lack an inherent ability to connect actions with outcomes.)

–I want to be able to afford to go to France this summer.

*What are the upsides and the downsides?
(Now together, you are beginning to assess risk levels, coaching them to detach a bit from the action and determine whether or not it is worth the time, effort or money. The key here is that you have not decided for them or manipulated them into your outcome but have coached them through the decision making process.)

–I'll make enough money to go on the trip, and have spending money while I'm there, and maybe even be able to put some in the bank for next year.

But trying to juggle two jobs and school might be too much-I might not be able to handle it. I don't want my grades to suffer because then I might loose my scholarship.

CHAPTER EIGHT

Miscellaneous Challenges

by Barbara Rhode, M.S., L.M.F.T.

"What lies behind us and what lies ahead of us are tiny matters compared to what lies within us."

–Thoreau

B ecause every parent, child, and situation is different, you won't all face the same challenges. The launching period may be easier for some and nightmarish for others. But there are some universal challenges that you will be better able to face if you know they're coming.

Cutting the (phone) cord

Cell phones and email have shortened distances between us dramatically, which can be positive or negative, depending on how you use them. Some people refer to cell phones as cordless tethers or electronic leashes.

These communication tools can be particularly problematic in the hands of what colleges term "helicopter parents" – those who continue to hover over their newly launched young adults. These parents think nothing of calling RA's, administrative staff or faculty when they feel that their son or daughter has not been treated fairly. Some major corporations are even warning employees to beware of parents who demand to be included in their college graduate's interview process.

Some campuses have opened, "Departments of Parental Affairs" to deal with this new development; and others are hiring seasoned, older students or RA's to gently intercede or redirect parents who are having trouble separating from the child or the situation. You do not want to be known as one of the parents who require this special handling!

Some parents call their student multiple times a day to "check" on them. In these cases, the umbilical cord hasn't been severed or even adequately stretched. The cord has just reworked itself into a new, electronic version that now reflects parental fears about letting go.

We know that young adults find it easier to communicate through email, and may become downright chatty during a cell phone call. I learned more about my teenage daughter through the emails she sent during her summer trip abroad than I did in all her high school years put together.

But as coaches, whenever we initiate contact with our newly launched child, we have to question our motive. Am I calling to check up or to make a connection? Who is this really about? Whose need is being met? If you want to call to see if they made their doctor's appointment or went to that early class, resist the urge. Making it to class or an appointment is their responsibility now, and missing it is their consequence, not yours.

When is it okay to call? We can define 'reasonable contact' as making weekly or bi-weekly calls; returning their phone calls; and calling to get necessary information, i.e., "Did you get the check I sent?" or "What time should I pick you up at the airport?"

You're in it together

Making sure your marriage doesn't take a back seat to launching your young adult can also pose challenges. It's a well-documented fact that marital satisfaction drops while we are busy raising teenagers. The teen years are ripe for conflict, and many couples find themselves pitted against each other regularly. Some children are naturally skilled at polarizing mom and dad, keeping things in a constant state of chaos. Couples may lose sight of each other, becoming focused on juggling the household while letting go of their own emotional intimacy.

My husband and I have made a 20-year practice of taking Friday nights off for ourselves. Since our children were born, we have routinely left them with family, babysitters and then on their own so that we can go off every Friday and spend some time alone. I look back now and believe that this faithful practice has done more for the ongoing health of our relationship than anything else. It has given us the time and energy to consistently take stock of our relationship and make the necessary changes to keep it thriving and maturing.

If you've put your relationship on hold until the kids are grown and out of the house, it's not too late to put it back on the front burner. It will take some time and effort because an intimate relationship is like any living thing – it needs to be nourished. If you've starved yours for years, you can't expect everything to be the way you want it to be right away. Now might be a good time to invest in some relationship counseling or pick up one of the books I have recommended in the bibliography to get started on rebuilding and refreshing your marriage.

Make yourself a priority

You may be juggling the teen years and launching with another major life event – taking care of aging parents. That would make you what author, Barbara Sher, calls "...the lost generation. We have kids who forget to call us and parents who don't remember us."

When you're stuck in the middle of conflicting demands, you may begin to wonder if there is anything left of you at the end of the day. Although it is true that, "this too shall pass," it can feel like an exhausting, "no end in sight" time of your life.

If you are part of this sandwich generation, try to give yourself some much-deserved breaks and don't forget to ask for help when you feel overwhelmed. Practice being extra kind to yourself, your partner, and other family members. Exercise, eat healthy, get enough sleep, take walks, and speak to family members the way you would speak to anyone else – with kindness and respect.

Single parents can experience a unique sense of loss during this developmental stage because children in single parent households often take on the role of companion. This is a good time to take stock, and invest time, energy and effort into redeveloping who you are. Now that you're not devoting all of what's left of you at the end of a workday to your child, new personal relationships become more feasible.

If you have other children who've been standing in the wings during the launch of their sibling, they, too, feel the effects of this transition. Many of them have stood by patiently, or not so patiently, while their high school senior sibling demanded so much of your time and attention. This can become their time, now that the nest is a little more spacious.

Like any other life transition, we can work at making this a positive one or we can shut down and fill the void with fear and pain. We always have the choice. No matter what the circumstances, we are in control of how we view this change and how we handle ourselves throughout the process.

EXERCISE

Take some time to think and discuss the following questions – in the car, after dinner, alone or with your spouse.

1. On a scale of 1 to 10, how satisfied are you with your personal life right now?
2. Where does your own wellness fall on your priority list?
3. What changes are you willing to make to improve that area of your life?
4. What one thing different can you do today to improve it? Now….go ahead and do it!

CHAPTER TEN

New Roles for All the Family

by Annette Reiter, M.A, L.M.F.T.

"We cannot direct the wind ... but we can adjust the sails."
                                                    –Anonymous

Parenting is the only job I know of where you eventually get fired for doing a great job. Be thankful for this pink slip – you worked very hard to get it.

But what are you really getting fired from? More importantly, what's next? As in all transitional phases of life, you're laying the groundwork for the future. During and after the launch of your young adult, it's critical to find new ways of connecting as you create a new family model.

I have a good friend with two adult children who constantly reminds me that the best time with her children is now. She notes that their relationship includes minimal worries and responsibilities on her part. She simply gets to enjoy their company while watching them turn into their own people – which I'm sure sounds pretty good to you right about now.

The families that adjust well to change and report less stress during the launching period are those who create new boundaries while balancing career and personal needs. On the other hand, high parental anxiety levels or significant emotional reactions to this roller coaster period can hinder independent development.

A family framework of trust, autonomy, competency, self-esteem and hope will make the ride through this transition period more pleasant and the outcomes more successful.

Adjusting to a new parenting style of coaching, encouraging and modeling will decrease stress for parents as they turn over responsibility to their children. Parents eventually enjoy the pleasures of watching their child's careers, relationships and lives blossom.

When thinking back on the hard work and years of parenting you've already put in, too many parents focus on their regrets or their perceived failures. Parents are designed to fail on some level, which adult children then have the chance to fix. If parents didn't fail somewhere how would any of us ever know we could do it on our own? No parent sets out to mess up his or her kids, and this shouldn't be a time of self-blame. Try accolades instead. If you can't let go of the blame, try repeating, "It's his life. It's her life." You're not in power any more, and you shouldn't be.

Independence was one of our founding fathers' values, and it's also a goal we share with our children. As our children launch toward independence, we remind ourselves that there will be some separation, but also reconnection in a more mature manner.

Let go of the special time of parenting young children, when you were magic to them. Embrace the fun of flaunting your flaws and exchanging mature love with your young adult. The future may hold exotic family vacations, heated political debates, exciting careers, blessings of partnership, grandchildren…who knows what else. It's time to sit back, relax and prepare to enjoy your pink slip.

"Should you shield the canyons from the windstorms, you would never see the beauty of their carvings."

–Elizabeth Kubler-Ross

BIBLIOGRAPHY

AmericanCatholic.org. <u>Messenger</u> publication, August 2002.

Arp, Dave. <u>Fighting For Your Empty Nest</u>. San Francisco, CA: Jossey-Bass, 2000.

Beattie, Melody. <u>Codependent No More</u>. New York, NY: Harper/Hazelden, 1987.

Bernstein, Mark and Yadin Kaufmann. <u>How to Survive Your Freshman Year</u>. Atlanta, GA: Hundred of Heads, 2004.

Bradley, Michael. <u>Yes, Your Teen is Crazy</u>. Gig Harbor, WA: Harbor Press, 2002.

Butler, K. "Teen Brain Drain." <u>St. Petersburg Times</u>. 9 July 2006.

Byron, Katie and Stephen Mitchell. <u>Loving What Is</u>. New York: Harmony Books, 2002.

Carter, Elizabeth and Monica McGoldrick. <u>The Changing Family Life Cycle</u>. Boston, MA: Allyn and Bacon, 1989.

Coburn, Karen and Madge Lawrence Treeger. <u>Letting Go, A Parents Guide to Understanding the College Years</u>. New York, NY: Quill, 2003.

Cormier, Robert. "<u>A Bad Time For Fathers</u>", Fiction, Laurel Leaf Publishing Paperback, March 1991, From collection "<u>8 + 1</u>".

Covey, Sean. <u>The 7 Habits of Highly Effective Teens</u>. New York: Simon and Schuster, 1998.

Dinkmeyer, Don and Gary McKay. <u>Systematic Training for Effective Parenting</u>. Circle Pines, Minn: American Guidance Services, 1989.

Fee, Susan. "My Roommate is Driving Me Crazy!" Adams Media, 2005.

Hesman, T and M. Franck. "Teen Brains: Volatile and Vulnerable." St. Petersburg Times. 1 January, 2006.

Hodges, Felicia. "Coping With an Empty Nest" Teenagers Today Website <http://teenagerstoday.com/resources/articles/emptynest.htm>

Hollowell, Dr.Edward. Crazy Busy. Ballentine Books, New York, 2006.

Johnson, Helen. Don't Tell Me What To Do, Just Send Money. New York: St. Martins Griffin, 2000.

Kantrowitz, B. and P. Tyre. "The Fine Art of Letting Go." Newsweek. 22 May 2006.

Megan, Kathleen "Touching Off Teen Tantrums." St. Petersburg Times. 28 December 2004.

PBS "Interview with Dr. Charles Nelson." PBS Frontline. 21 Dec. 2005 <http://www.pbs.org/wgbh/ages/frontline/shows/teenbrain/>

PBS "Interview with Dr. Walter Norvell." PBS Frontline. 21 Dec. 2005 <http://www.pbs.org/wgbh/pages/frontline/shows/teenbrain/>

Phylameana Lila Desy. "Empty Nest Revisited" , Holistic Healing Website at About.com <http://healing.about.com/cs/emptynest/a/emptynestrv.htm>

Putnam, Robert D. Bowling Alone. Simon & Schuster Paperbacks, New York, 2000.

Reznick, Charlotte. "Emotional Intelligence: What is It, Who Has It, and How to Get It." Imagery for Kids. 21 Dec. 2005 <http://www.imageryforkids.com/>

Twenge, Jean M. <u>Generation Me.</u> Free Press, New York, 2006.

Quinn, Jane Bryant. "Money Guide: A Cash Course for Kids".
<u>Newsweek.</u> September 12, 2005.

Tolle, Eckart. <u>The Power of Now</u>. Novato, CA: New World Library,
1999.

Walsh, David. <u>Why Do They Act That Way</u>. New York: Free Press,
2004.

Yale Health Care, Vol. VI,No.5, Sept-Oct. 2003.

ABOUT THE AUTHORS

Barbara Rhode is a licensed marriage and family therapist with over 25 years of clinical experience. She has presented workshops locally and nationally and is also a consultant for Military OneSource, providing clinical assessments and services to the military and their families throughout the world. Barbara writes a monthly column for the St. Petersburg Times on a variety of relationship and wellness issues. She is a wife and mother of three.

Annette Reiter is a licensed marriage and family therapist who manages a private practice in downtown St. Petersburg, FL. In addition to graduating from the University of San Diego, she has co-authored 2 books on parenting, written several journal articles, a blog on Parenting, and has spoken at the National Conference of American Association of Marriage and Family Therapists. She currently lives with her husband of 16 years, their daughter, dog and cat. Her hobbies include reading, gardening, making cheese and volunteering at her daughter's school.

Barbara and Annette have presented a variety of workshops including:

Launching Your Adolescent into Healthy Adulthood
The Truth & Lies about Texting Teens
Preparing Your Child for the College Experience
Compassion Fatigue – The Cost of Caring
Understanding & Changing Emotional Eating Patterns

For additional information, please contact:

Barbara Rhode, LMFT (MT1364)
brhode840@hotmail.com

Annette Reiter, MA, LMFT (MT 1896)
www.StPetersburgTherapy.com

CPSIA information can be obtained
at www.ICGtesting.com
Printed in the USA
FFHW020603130719
53608505-59297FF

9 781600 474118